Predators

GRAY WOLVES

BY LIBBY WILSON

WWW.APEXEDITIONS.COM

Copyright © 2024 by Apex Editions, Mendota Heights, MN 55120. All rights reserved. No part of this book may be reproduced or utilized in any form or by any means without written permission from the publisher.

Apex is distributed by North Star Editions:
sales@northstareditions.com | 888-417-0195

Produced for Apex by Red Line Editorial.

Photographs©: iStockphoto, cover, 4–5, 7, 10–11, 19, 29; Shutterstock Images, 1, 6, 8, 12, 13, 14–15, 16–17, 18, 20–21, 22–23, 25, 26–27

Library of Congress Control Number: 2023910142

ISBN
978-1-63738-772-6 (hardcover)
978-1-63738-815-0 (paperback)
978-1-63738-896-9 (ebook pdf)
978-1-63738-858-7 (hosted ebook)

Printed in the United States of America
Mankato, MN
012024

NOTE TO PARENTS AND EDUCATORS

Apex books are designed to build literacy skills in striving readers. Exciting, high-interest content attracts and holds readers' attention. The text is carefully leveled to allow students to achieve success quickly. Additional features, such as bolded glossary words for difficult terms, help build comprehension.

TABLE OF CONTENTS

CHAPTER 1
ON THE HUNT 4

CHAPTER 2
A WOLF'S WORLD 10

CHAPTER 3
WOLF PACKS 16

CHAPTER 4
CATCHING PREY 22

COMPREHENSION QUESTIONS • 28
GLOSSARY • 30
TO LEARN MORE • 31
ABOUT THE AUTHOR • 31
INDEX • 32

CHAPTER 1
ON THE HUNT

A pack of gray wolves circle a bison. The wolves snap and snarl. Their last meal was days ago.

Wolves sometimes go more than a week without eating.

A male bison can weigh up to 2,000 pounds (900 kg).

The huge bison paws at the ground. It bellows a loud warning. Then it swings its horns. The wolves decide not to attack.

TESTING PREY

Wolves often hunt animals much larger than themselves. That can be **dangerous**. Wolves can be hurt or killed. So, they test their **prey**. If an animal is strong, the pack finds weaker prey.

When hunting, wolves often surround their prey and attack from all sides.

The pack searches for easier prey. They chase a group of deer. One of the deer lags behind the rest. The wolves attack and eat it.

FAST FACT
Wolves have sharp teeth and strong jaws. Their bites can break bones.

◀ Wolves often separate an animal from a group before killing it.

CHAPTER 2

A WOLF'S WORLD

Gray wolves are powerful **predators**. Most live in northern parts of the world. Gray wolves can live in forests, mountains, grasslands, or deserts.

Gray wolves live in parts of North America, Europe, and Asia.

Large paws help wolves run easily on snow.

Wolves have **adapted** to cold places. Their thick fur has two layers. A fluffy undercoat traps heat. Long outer hairs block water.

SEA WOLVES

Some gray wolves live by the ocean. These wolves often hunt salmon. But they only eat the salmons' heads. That helps them avoid **diseases** from the fish.

Some gray wolves live near the coast of Canada.

Wolves' senses help them hunt and stay safe. Wolves can hear sounds up to 10 miles (16 km) away. And they can see well in the dark.

FAST FACT

A gray wolf's sense of smell is 100 times better than a human's.

A wolf's eyes are good at spotting quick movements.

CHAPTER 3

WOLF PACKS

Gray wolves live in family packs. Each pack has its own **territory**. Wolves mark their territory with scents. The smells warn other packs to stay away.

Most packs have 6 to 10 wolves. A few large packs may reach 30 or more.

Usually, one male and one female lead the pack. These leaders have babies. The rest of the wolves help raise them. They guard the pups and teach them to hunt.

Female wolves usually have four to six pups at a time.

Pack members feed the pups by spitting up into their mouths.

BODY TALK

Wolves howl to **communicate**. They also use their bodies. Leaders stand tall with their tails high. Followers crouch and tuck their tails. These postures show who's in charge.

A wolf can travel hundreds of miles when searching for a mate.

After a year, young wolves are fully grown. By age three, they often leave the pack. They find **mates** and start their own packs.

FAST FACT
Most wild wolves live between six and eight years.

CHAPTER 4

CATCHING PREY

Gray wolves often eat elk, moose, and deer. But they hunt smaller animals, too. They will also eat plants or dead animals.

Gray wolves are apex predators. That means no other animals hunt them.

Wolves usually hunt in packs. They follow prey over long distances. Then they work together to kill it.

FAST FACT

For short times, wolves can run more than 35 miles per hour (56 km/h).

Wolves can travel as much as 30 miles (48 km) in one day when following prey.

Some wolves run ahead. They stop the prey from getting away. Others bite the prey's neck or shoulders. Their sharp teeth help bring the animal down.

The wolves in a pack share food with one another. But they guard their kills from other animals.

BIG MEALS

Most wolf packs catch less than one-fourth of the animals they chase. When wolves do make a kill, they eat as much as possible. A large wolf can eat up to 22 pounds (10 kg) of food in one meal.

COMPREHENSION QUESTIONS

Write your answers on a separate piece of paper.

1. Write a few sentences describing how wolves hunt.

2. What fact about gray wolves is most interesting to you? Why?

3. Which layer of a wolf's fur traps heat?
    - A. the fluffy undercoat
    - B. the long outer hairs
    - C. the short outer hairs

4. Why would wolves eat as much as possible after making a kill?
    - A. They can only catch small animals.
    - B. They will eat again a short time later.
    - C. Their next kill might be a long time later.

5. What does **scents** mean in this book?

*Wolves mark their territory with **scents**. The smells warn other packs to stay away.*

    A. groups of animals
    B. types of smells
    C. times of day

6. What does **postures** mean in this book?

*Leaders stand tall with their tails high. Followers crouch and tuck their tails. These **postures** show who's in charge.*

    A. ways of moving the body
    B. ways of making sound
    C. ways of telling time

Answer key on page 32.

GLOSSARY

adapted
Changed to fit a particular situation.

communicate
To send and receive messages.

dangerous
Likely to cause problems or harm.

diseases
Sicknesses.

mates
Pairs of animals that come together to have babies.

predators
Animals that hunt and eat other animals.

prey
Animals that are hunted and eaten by other animals.

territory
An area that an animal or group of animals lives in and defends.

TO LEARN MORE

BOOKS

Albertson, Al. *Gray Wolves*. Minneapolis: Bellwether Media, 2020.

Borgert-Spaniol, Megan. *Gray Wolves: Yellowstone's Hunters*. Minneapolis: Abdo Publishing, 2020.

Markle, Sandra. *On the Hunt with Wolves*. Minneapolis: Lerner Publications, 2023.

ONLINE RESOURCES

Visit **www.apexeditions.com** to find links and resources related to this title.

ABOUT THE AUTHOR

Libby Wilson is a retired librarian who has loved books all her life. She loves to research and learn amazing facts to share with readers. Her favorite topics to write about are animals, history, and inspirational people.

INDEX

B
bison, 4, 6

D
deer, 9, 22
diseases, 13

E
elk, 22

F
forests, 10
fur, 12

G
grasslands, 10

J
jaws, 9

M
mates, 21
moose, 22
mountains, 10

O
ocean, 13

P
pack, 4, 7, 9, 16, 18, 21, 24, 27
predators, 10

S
salmon, 13

T
teeth, 9, 26
territory, 16

ANSWER KEY:
1. Answers will vary; 2. Answers will vary; 3. A; 4. C; 5. B; 6. A